Why was Charles Spurgeon called a prince?

Thuy Vu

Why was Charles Spurgeon called a Prince?
Text and Illustration Copyright by Thuy Vu
Published: October 2014

ISBN-13: 978-1502905406
ISBN-10: 150290540X

All rights reserved. No part of this publication may be reproduced, stored in a retrieval system, or transmitted in any form or by any means – electronic, mechanical, photocopy, recording, or any other – except for brief quotations in printed reviews, without the prior permission of the author.
You must not circulate this book in any format.

Who was Charles Spurgeon?
And why was he known
as the Prince of Preachers --
if he never wore a crown?

Not to king or duke or baron
but to a preacher rather poor
was born little boy Spurgeon
in the year 1834.

He grew up loving to read
books of all kinds,
especially *The Pilgrim's Progress*
which he read a hundred times!

He was quite a stubborn boy
who might have gone astray,
were it not for his mom
who ceaselessly would pray.

Under the weight of daily sin
he felt so stained and dirty.
How could a God so pure
love someone so unworthy?

And thus he questioned loudly
in his thoughts throughout the day.
Until at age fifteen,
a storm got in the way.

Caught in a heavy blizzard
with nowhere warm to go,
Spurgeon spotted a little church
and tramped there through the snow.

He stepped inside the church
and beheld before his eyes:
a simple man was preaching
on Isaiah forty-five.

"Look upon me and be ye saved!"
The man quoted in unlearned fashion.
He even mispronounced some words
but spoke with fervent passion.

Then the preacher pointed to Spurgeon
who looked so sad and pitiful,
"You there, young man,
Are looking very miserable!"

"You have nothin' to do but look and live!
Look to Christ!" he pleaded.
Suddenly Spurgeon saw
the salvation of God:
JESUS was all he needed!

Spurgeon looked and looked
and looked
on Jesus bright as day.
Not one thing more
had to be done
to take his sins away.

Such freedom caused him joy to speak
of love so sweet and glorious.
It led him down the road to preach
a gospel so victorious.

At a tiny chapel in Waterbeach,
Spurgeon taught the word of God.
The attendance grew and grew and grew,
and those who heard were awed.

Then New Park Street Chapel learned
of this boy with gifted tongue.
They asked him to be their pastor
at only twenty years young!

It was the largest Baptist church in London;
every week, a thousand came.
Through Spurgeon's sermons tens
of thousands more
would trust in Jesus' name.

He once preached to twenty-three
thousand people
without a microphone!
It was proof of God's great work,
and he credited Him alone.

Spurgeon married his dear Susannah
who was a wife supportive and true.
Together they had twin sons
who would become pastors too!

He wrote books, articles and sermons
and created a Pastors' College.
He cared for little boys and girls
by starting an orphanage.

So you see...

he was called
the Prince of Preachers
for so gifted was he
among the Church's teachers.

He never wore a glittering crown
or donned a golden fleece.
But he DID use all his days
to worship
the True Prince of Peace!

"You cannot be Christ's servant if you
are not willing to follow him, cross and all.
What do you crave?
A crown?
Then it must be a crown of thorns
if you are to be like him.
Do you want to be lifted up?
So you shall, but it will be upon a cross."

-Charles Haddon Spurgeon

Made in the USA
Las Vegas, NV
31 May 2022